ISBN: 9798883740335
Imprint: Independently published

Cover design by: Art Painter
Library of Congress Control Number: 2018675309
Printed in the United States of America

"In the tapestry of audacity, each thread of innovation weaves a narrative that transcends the ordinary. Mavericks are not merely dreamers; they are the architects of possibility, crafting a symphony of disruption that resonates through the corridors of time."

CHIMEZIE IGWE

CONTENTS

PREFACE

A Journey into Audacious Entrepreneurship

Welcome to the prelude of a journey into the dynamic and transformative realm of maverick entrepreneurship. In the pages that follow, we embark on an exploration of audacity, innovation, and the indomitable spirit that defines those who dare to break free from the ordinary and shape the extraordinary.

Setting the Stage:
In the preface, we set the stage for an odyssey that transcends conventional boundaries. The entrepreneurial landscape is a canvas upon which mavericks paint with bold strokes, crafting narratives that challenge norms, disrupt industries, and leave an indelible mark on the world. This exploration is not just a chronicle of business success; it is an immersion into the mindset that propels audacious thinkers into the vanguard of transformative change.

Defining the Maverick Mindset:
As we delve into the core of maverick entrepreneurship, the preface unveils the essence of the Maverick Mindset. It is a mindset that defies conformity, embraces risk with strategic intent, and envisions possibilities beyond the horizon. Mavericks are not content with the status quo; they are architects of change, driven by a relentless pursuit of innovation that reshapes

industries and influences society.

An Invitation to Audacity:
The preface extends an invitation to the readers—an invitation to embrace audacity. It beckons dreamers, aspiring entrepreneurs, and those hungry for inspiration to join in the exploration of a mindset that shatters limitations and redefines what is possible. Mavericks are not bound by the ordinary; they navigate uncharted territories, fueled by the audacious belief that their ideas can transform the world.

Guiding Principles:
Within these introductory pages, we lay the foundation for the guiding principles that will unfold in the subsequent chapters. From disruptive innovation to strategic risk-taking, from the power of storytelling to adaptive leadership, the preface introduces the themes that will illuminate the journey ahead. These principles form the pillars of the Maverick Mindset, shaping the narrative of audacious entrepreneurship.

An Inspirational Prelude:
The preface serves as an inspirational prelude—a glimpse into the stories of mavericks who have left an indelible mark on the entrepreneurial landscape. It hints at the societal impact, the audacious endeavors, and the transformative journeys that will unfold in the chapters to come. Through these pages, readers are invited to witness and internalize the audacity that propels mavericks forward.

The Unveiling:
As we conclude the preface, the stage is set, and the curtain rises on a journey into the heart of audacious entrepreneurship. Mavericks Unveiled is not just a narrative; it is an immersive experience, an exploration that invites readers to not only witness the audacity of mavericks but to internalize the mindset that propels them to break boundaries and build empires.

Welcome to a journey where audacity is not a choice but a guiding principle, where innovation is not a luxury but a necessity, and where the extraordinary is not an exception but a way of life. Welcome to Mavericks Unveiled—a celebration of audacious thinking and transformative impact. The journey begins here, and the pages that follow await the curious minds ready to embrace the Maverick Mindset.

INTRODUCTION
The Maverick Entrepreneur - Pioneering Paths to Uncharted Success

Welcome, dear reader, to a journey into the riveting world of entrepreneurial mavericks. In the fast-paced realm of business, where norms are challenged and boundaries are shattered, this exploration invites you to navigate the stories of visionaries who dared to defy convention, building empires that echo through the corridors of innovation.

In the grand tapestry of business, mavericks stand out as vibrant threads, weaving tales of audacity and creativity. Picture this: a lone individual, armed with an idea that defies tradition, strides into the uncharted territories of entrepreneurship. What propels them forward? What sets these individuals apart in a landscape crowded with conformity?

Let's embark on this exploration with the understanding that maverick entrepreneurs are not just disruptors; they are architects of change, sculpting new possibilities from the clay of the status quo. As we unravel their stories, we'll be delving into the very essence of what makes a maverick tick and the profound impact their journeys have on the world of business.

Consider the pioneers who laid the groundwork for maverick thinking. Think back to the trailblazers who transformed industries, questioning the established norms, and left an indelible mark on business history. These stories are not just about financial success; they are about the spirit of innovation, resilience, and the unyielding belief that a single idea has the power to revolutionize.

Now, let's journey to the present, where maverick entrepreneurs continue to redefine success on their own terms. We'll immerse ourselves in the narratives of those who refused to color within the lines, opting instead to paint their masterpieces on blank canvases. Their ventures are not just businesses; they are living organisms, breathing life into concepts that challenge the ordinary.

As we traverse through these stories, you'll encounter the Maverick Mindset - an elusive yet powerful force that propels individuals beyond the boundaries of conventional thinking. It's not just about risk-taking; it's about calculated daring. It's not just about disruption; it's about constructive revolution. The maverick mindset is the heartbeat of our exploration, pulsating with energy and the promise of transformative insights.

To truly understand the maverick entrepreneur, we must delve into the toolkit that sets them apart. From unconventional marketing strategies to innovative leadership approaches, each tool is carefully selected to carve a unique niche in the competitive business landscape. Think of this toolkit as a symphony of tactics, harmonizing to create a melody that resonates with consumers and disrupts industries.

Now, let's address the challenges that mavericks willingly face. For every success story, there are hurdles to overcome, setbacks to navigate, and storms to weather. Yet, what makes these entrepreneurs truly remarkable is their resilience - a resilience that transforms obstacles into stepping stones, failures into lessons, and challenges into opportunities.

But, the impact of maverick entrepreneurs extends beyond the boardroom. They are not just architects of businesses; they are sculptors of societal change. We'll examine how these visionaries influence culture, challenge norms, and contribute to the societal tapestry in ways that reverberate far beyond profit margins.

As we explore the stories of these mavericks, we'll also turn our attention to the aspirants, those who dream of joining the ranks of the unconventional trailblazers. For those yearning to cultivate an entrepreneurial spirit, this exploration serves as a guide, offering valuable insights and a roadmap to embrace the Maverick Mindset.

In this comprehensive journey, we will not only celebrate the success stories but also dissect the failures, extracting lessons that add depth to our understanding of maverick entrepreneurship. Each narrative is a lesson, each insight a gem, and each challenge a stepping stone toward uncharted success.

So, fasten your seatbelt as we venture into the pages of "The Maverick Entrepreneur: Breaking Boundaries, Building Empires." This isn't just a book; it's an odyssey into the extraordinary, where the human spirit converges with business acumen to create a narrative that transcends the ordinary. Onward we sail, ready to be inspired, challenged, and transformed by the stories of those who dared to be mavericks in the world of business.

CHAPTER 1
Mavericks in History

In the annals of business history, certain individuals emerge as titans, not merely for their financial triumphs, but for their audacious spirit and paradigm-shifting ideas. These are the mavericks, the trailblazers who, throughout time, defied conventions and left an indelible mark on the entrepreneurial landscape.

Let's rewind the clock to an era where innovation wasn't just a buzzword but a way of life. Our journey begins with a closer look at historical figures whose entrepreneurial spirits blazed a trail for future mavericks. These were the visionaries who saw beyond the constraints of their times, laying the foundation for the maverick mindset that continues to shape businesses today.

Consider the tale of Andrew Carnegie, a steel magnate whose audacity and strategic thinking transformed an entire industry. In the late 19th century, as others clung to traditional methods, Carnegie embraced innovation, revolutionizing steel production and leaving an indomitable legacy. His story is a testament to the power of visionary thinking, illustrating that maverick entrepreneurs are not bound by the norms of their era but are architects of change.

Moving forward, let's examine the life and times of Coco Chanel, a maverick in the world of fashion. In an era dominated by corsets and rigid fashion norms, Chanel dared to challenge the status quo. Her introduction of casual, comfortable clothing for women revolutionized the fashion industry, demonstrating that mavericks are not confined to specific sectors; they emerge wherever norms are ripe for disruption.

The journey wouldn't be complete without acknowledging the contributions of a modern visionary, Steve Jobs. Co-founder of Apple Inc., Jobs transformed the way we interact with technology, forever altering the trajectory of personal computing. His story is more than a Silicon Valley legend; it's a testament to the maverick's ability to envision the future and relentlessly pursue innovation, even in the face of skepticism.

These historical mavericks share a common thread – a refusal to adhere to the status quo and an unwavering belief in the power of their ideas. Their stories serve as beacons, illuminating the path for future generations of entrepreneurs to venture into uncharted territories.

As we embark on this exploration of mavericks in history, let's not merely recount their successes, but delve into the mindset that propelled them to greatness. What drove them to challenge the norms of their time? How did they navigate adversity and turn setbacks into stepping stones? These are the questions that will guide our journey into the heart of what it means to be a maverick entrepreneur.

Join me as we step into the footprints of those who dared to be different, charting a course through history to unravel the secrets of the maverick mindset. Through their stories, we'll uncover the timeless principles that continue to shape the entrepreneurial landscape and inspire the trailblazers of tomorrow. Onward we go, into the first chapter of "The Maverick Entrepreneur: Breaking Boundaries, Building Empires."

CHAPTER 2
Defying Conventions: The Maverick Mindset

In the vast tapestry of entrepreneurship, the Maverick Mindset emerges as the guiding force behind individuals who dare to challenge conventions and forge their own paths. It's not merely a set of principles; it's a way of thinking that propels maverick entrepreneurs beyond the boundaries of the ordinary.

THE MAVERICK'S VISION

At the core of the Maverick Mindset lies an unwavering vision that transcends immediate circumstances. Mavericks see beyond what is to what could be, envisioning possibilities that elude the conventional thinker. Take the example of Elon Musk, whose vision extends beyond creating successful businesses to transforming entire industries, from electric cars to space travel. The Maverick's vision is expansive, fueled by a belief that the status quo is merely a starting point.

CALCULATED DARING

Daring is a word often associated with maverick entrepreneurs, but it's not reckless abandon; it's calculated daring. Mavericks understand risk but are not paralyzed by it. Instead, they embrace risk as an inherent part of the entrepreneurial journey. Consider the calculated risks taken by Richard Branson, who turned the music industry on its head with Virgin Records and later ventured into space tourism with Virgin Galactic. The Maverick's approach to risk is strategic, a willingness to push boundaries while maintaining a keen awareness of potential outcomes.

INNOVATIVE THINKING

Innovation is the lifeblood of the Maverick Mindset. Mavericks thrive on pushing the boundaries of what is known and accepted, consistently seeking novel solutions to challenges. Steve Jobs, with his focus on user-friendly design and groundbreaking technology, exemplifies this commitment to innovation. The Maverick's mind is a breeding ground for creative disruption, where new ideas are not just welcomed but actively pursued.

RESILIENCE IN THE FACE OF FAILURE

Failure is not the end for a maverick; it's a stepping stone to success. Mavericks understand that setbacks are part of the entrepreneurial journey and view failure as an opportunity to learn and iterate. The story of Oprah Winfrey, who faced numerous challenges on her path to media mogul status, showcases the resilience ingrained in the Maverick Mindset. Rather than succumbing to failure, mavericks use it as a catalyst for growth.

UNCONVENTIONAL LEADERSHIP

Maverick entrepreneurs often adopt leadership styles that defy traditional norms. They inspire through bold action, authenticity, and a willingness to challenge hierarchical structures. Consider the leadership style of Jack Ma, founder of Alibaba, who champions a flat organizational structure and values individual empowerment. The Maverick's leadership is inclusive, fostering a culture where ideas are valued, and individuals are encouraged to think independently.

As we delve into the Maverick Mindset, let's not only explore these principles but also reflect on how they can be applied in our own entrepreneurial journeys. Maverick entrepreneurs are not born; they are shaped by their mindset, a mindset that can be cultivated and embraced by those willing to defy conventions and challenge the status quo.

Join me in unlocking the secrets of the Maverick Mindset, understanding how it shapes the decisions, actions, and ultimate success of those who refuse to be bound by the ordinary. Onward we go, into the heart of unconventional thinking, ready to embrace the transformative power of the Maverick Mindset in the second chapter of "The Maverick Entrepreneur: Breaking Boundaries, Building Empires."

CHAPTER 3
Mavericks on the Rise: Inspirational Profiles

As we continue our expedition into the world of maverick entrepreneurship, Chapter 3 opens a treasure trove of contemporary narratives, showcasing the lives and ventures of modern mavericks who have not only broken boundaries but have become beacons of inspiration for the aspiring entrepreneur.

ELON MUSK: THE BOUNDARY BENDER

No exploration of modern mavericks would be complete without delving into the audacious ventures of Elon Musk. From revolutionizing online payments with PayPal to pushing the automotive industry's boundaries with Tesla and transforming space travel through SpaceX, Musk epitomizes the relentless pursuit of groundbreaking innovation. His story is a testament to the maverick's ability to envision the future and manifest it through unwavering determination.

ARIANNA HUFFINGTON: REDEFINING SUCCESS

In a world often measured by financial metrics, Arianna Huffington stands as a maverick who challenges the traditional definition of success. Co-founder of The Huffington Post, she redirected her focus to redefine success through the lens of well-being with Thrive Global. Huffington's journey reflects the maverick's capacity to question prevailing norms and pivot toward a more holistic vision of accomplishment.

JEFF BEZOS: FROM BOOKSELLER TO SPACE PIONEER

Jeff Bezos, the founder of Amazon, has transformed the landscape of retail and digital technology. His journey from an online bookseller to the visionary behind one of the world's largest e-commerce and cloud computing platforms illustrates the maverick's ability to adapt, innovate, and diversify. Bezos's venture into space exploration with Blue Origin further solidifies his maverick status, showcasing a relentless pursuit of groundbreaking endeavors.

CHER WANG: TECH TRAILBLAZER

Cher Wang, co-founder of HTC Corporation and a trailblazer in the tech industry, exemplifies how mavericks can thrive in traditionally male-dominated sectors. Her innovative approach to mobile technology and commitment to pushing the boundaries of what's possible showcase the transformative power of the maverick mindset. Wang's story inspires not only aspiring entrepreneurs but also challenges existing industry norms.

RICHARD BRANSON: MAVERICK ACROSS INDUSTRIES

Richard Branson, the founder of the Virgin Group, is a maverick whose ventures span a multitude of industries, from music to airlines to space tourism. His approach to business is characterized by a fearless spirit, an embrace of risk, and an unwavering belief in the power of entrepreneurship to drive positive change. Branson's ability to disrupt diverse markets underscores the versatility of the maverick mindset.

These modern mavericks share common threads: an unyielding belief in their visions, a capacity to pivot in the face of change, and a commitment to pushing the boundaries of what's possible. Their stories serve as both roadmaps and inspiration for those who dare to challenge norms and dream of leaving an indelible mark on the entrepreneurial landscape.

As we immerse ourselves in the inspirational profiles of these contemporary mavericks, let's not only celebrate their successes but also dissect the lessons embedded in their journeys. What can we glean from their approaches to innovation, adaptability, and resilience? Join me in the exploration of these maverick tales, where each narrative unfolds as a testament to the transformative power of daring to be different. Onward we go, ready to absorb the wisdom of those who have risen as modern entrepreneurial icons. Welcome to Chapter 3 of "The Maverick Entrepreneur: Breaking Boundaries, Building Empires."

CHAPTER 4
The Maverick's Toolkit: Strategies for Success

In the riveting landscape of maverick entrepreneurship, the journey toward success is not a mere happenstance but a meticulously crafted odyssey guided by a toolkit of strategies. Chapter 4 invites us to plunge into this toolkit, where each implement is a strategic instrument wielded by maverick entrepreneurs, propelling them beyond the realms of convention into the echelons of transformative success.

DISRUPTIVE INNOVATION: THE CATALYST OF CHANGE

At the nucleus of Maverick's Toolkit lies the force of disruptive innovation — a dynamic process that challenges established norms and reshapes entire industries. Take, for instance, the seismic impact of Netflix on the entertainment paradigm. By introducing streaming services, Netflix revolutionized how content is consumed, emphasizing that mavericks not only embrace innovation for novelty but strategically deploy it to redefine markets and consumer expectations.

In our exploration of disruptive innovation, we unveil how mavericks such as Elon Musk, the visionary founder of Tesla, transcend the automotive industry. Musk's commitment to electric vehicles and sustainable energy solutions is not merely a market strategy but a radical reimagining of transportation. Mavericks understand that innovation, when strategically applied, becomes a formidable weapon in their arsenal.

STRATEGIC RISK-TAKING: CALCULATED VENTURES INTO THE UNKNOWN

Risk is not a deterrent for mavericks; it's a calculated venture into the unknown. Chapter 4 delves into the art of strategic risk-taking as an integral component of Maverick's Toolkit. Examining the audacious acquisition strategies of Mark Zuckerberg, the innovative mind behind Facebook, showcases how calculated risks are not reckless gambles but deliberate maneuvers to secure transformative success.

Consider the realm of cryptocurrency, where Vitalik Buterin, the co-founder of Ethereum, embraced the risk of pioneering a decentralized blockchain platform. Mavericks comprehend that strategic risks are not just about embracing uncertainty but about paving new pathways in uncharted territories, where the potential for transformative impact outweighs the apprehension of the unknown.

BRAND AMBASSADORS AND STORYTELLERS: CRAFTING NARRATIVES THAT RESONATE

The Maverick's Toolkit extends beyond tangible products and services to the ethereal realm of branding and storytelling. Chapter 4 unveils how mavericks such as Elon Musk (Tesla) and Steve Jobs (Apple) transcend the traditional entrepreneurial role and become brand ambassadors and storytellers. Their ventures are not just businesses; they are narratives woven into the cultural fabric.

Musk, with his charismatic brand building, transforms Tesla into a symbol of sustainable innovation, while Jobs, with his storytelling prowess, elevates Apple beyond a tech company to an embodiment of design and innovation. Mavericks understand that effective storytelling transforms ventures into cultural phenomena, resonating not just with consumers but with society at large.

AGILE ADAPTATION: NAVIGATING THE SHIFTING TIDES

Adaptability is a cornerstone of Maverick's Toolkit, allowing entrepreneurs to navigate the ever-evolving landscapes of business. Chapter 4 explores the stories of adaptable mavericks like Jack Ma, who guided Alibaba through the dynamic e-commerce ecosystem. The Maverick's Toolkit includes the agility to adapt, ensuring that ventures not only survive but thrive amidst industry shifts.

As we delve into the world of adaptable mavericks, we witness the transformative power of flexibility in the face of change. Mavericks do not cling rigidly to initial strategies; instead, they pivot with grace, demonstrating that adaptability is not a sign of weakness but a strategic maneuver to seize emerging opportunities.

UNCONVENTIONAL LEADERSHIP STYLES: INSPIRING EXCELLENCE

Leadership is a linchpin in the Maverick's Toolkit, shaping organizational cultures and steering ventures toward success. Analyzing the diverse leadership styles of figures like Oprah Winfrey and Jeff Bezos unveils Maverick's approach to leadership — a departure from conventional norms that inspire loyalty, innovation, and resilience within organizations.

Winfrey's empowering leadership style fosters a culture of individual growth and empowerment, while Bezos's customer-centric ethos has transformed Amazon into an e-commerce giant. Mavericks understand that leadership is not a one-size-fits-all concept but an evolving, adaptable approach that aligns with the values and goals of their ventures.

INCLUSIVE DECISION-MAKING: HARNESSING THE POWER OF DIVERSITY

Inclusivity is a powerful tool in Maverick's Toolkit, amplifying decision-making processes with diverse perspectives. Examining the collaborative culture fostered by mavericks like Richard Branson showcases how a diversity of insights fuels innovation. The Maverick's Toolkit embraces inclusivity, ensuring that decisions are made with a breadth of perspectives and experiences.

Branson's commitment to a flat organizational structure and value for individual empowerment illustrates how mavericks leverage diversity to drive creativity and problem-solving. Inclusive decision-making is not just a checkbox in Maverick's Toolkit; it's a strategic advantage that propels ventures forward by tapping into a rich tapestry of perspectives.

As we explore Maverick's Toolkit, it becomes evident that each strategy is not an isolated entity but a thread intricately woven into the fabric of transformative success. The Maverick's Toolkit is a symphony, where disruptive innovation harmonizes with strategic risk-taking, storytelling resonates with agile adaptation, and inclusive decision-making orchestrates a culture of excellence.

Join me in this comprehensive exploration, where we not

only uncover the tools but understand how mavericks synergize them to construct a transformative force. Each tool serves a purpose, and each strategy complements another, together, they construct a framework for success that transcends the boundaries of conventional thinking.

Onward we go, armed with insights, inspiration, and a deeper understanding of the strategies that carve out empires in the entrepreneurial landscape. Welcome to Chapter 4 of "The Maverick Entrepreneur: Breaking Boundaries, Building Empires," where the Maverick's Toolkit unfolds as a comprehensive guide for those daring to be different in the world of business.

CHAPTER 5
Navigating Challenges:
Maverick Resilience

In the dynamic landscape of maverick entrepreneurship, success is not a smooth, unobstructed trajectory. It's a journey fraught with challenges, setbacks, and unforeseen obstacles. Chapter 5 illuminates the pivotal aspect of the Maverick's Toolkit: resilience. The ability to weather storms, navigate uncharted waters, and emerge stronger on the other side distinguishes maverick entrepreneurs from the ordinary.

RESILIENCE REDEFINED: THE MAVERICK'S FORTITUDE

Resilience in the Maverick's Toolkit is not merely about bouncing back from setbacks. It's a profound fortitude that transforms challenges into opportunities for growth. Mavericks understand that adversity is not an anomaly but an inherent part of the entrepreneurial journey. This chapter unravels stories of mavericks who faced with seemingly insurmountable challenges, exemplified resilience as a driving force.

Consider the narrative of Howard Schultz, the visionary behind Starbucks. Schultz faced rejection and skepticism when introducing the concept of premium coffee in a market saturated with traditional brews. His resilience, however, transformed Starbucks into a global phenomenon. Maverick views challenges not as roadblocks but as invitations to innovate, adapt, and evolve.

LEARNING FROM FAILURE: MAVERICKS EMBRACE SETBACKS

Failure, in the Maverick's Toolkit, is not a terminal point but a stepping stone toward success. Mavericks like J.K. Rowling, who faced numerous rejections before achieving literary stardom, demonstrate how setbacks can be transformative. This chapter delves into the narratives of entrepreneurs who embraced failure as a catalyst for learning, growth, and ultimately, triumph.

The Maverick's relationship with failure is nuanced; it's not a sign of inadequacy but an acknowledgment that experimentation involves inherent risks. Through vivid stories, we witness how mavericks like Henry Ford and Bill Gates navigated failures, refined their approaches, and emerged as industry titans.

ADAPTING TO INDUSTRY SHIFTS: MAVERICKS IN THE FACE OF CHANGE

Industries are not static entities; they evolve, pivot, and sometimes undergo seismic shifts. Mavericks recognize the inevitability of change and position themselves as adaptable architects of transformation. This chapter explores the stories of entrepreneurs like Angela Ahrendts, who navigated the retail industry through digital transformations at Burberry and later at Apple, showcasing Maverick's ability to anticipate and adapt to industry shifts.

Adaptability, in Maverick's Toolkit, is not a reactionary response but a proactive strategy to stay ahead of the curve. Mavericks remain vigilant to market dynamics, technological advancements, and shifts in consumer behavior, positioning themselves as pioneers rather than casualties of change.

THE MAVERICK MINDSET IN THE FACE OF CRITICISM: TURNING SKEPTICISM INTO FUEL

Mavericks often encounter skepticism and resistance, especially when challenging established norms. This chapter explores how mavericks turn criticism into fuel for innovation. The narrative of Sara Blakely, founder of Spanx, illustrates how she defied industry skepticism and reshaped the undergarment market. Maverick views criticism not as a deterrent but as motivation to prove the naysayers wrong.

The Maverick's Toolkit equips entrepreneurs with a mental resilience that transcends external skepticism. Mavericks understand that true innovation often elicits resistance, and instead of succumbing to doubt, they use it to fuel their determination. This chapter unveils the strategies mavericks employ to transform skepticism into a driving force for success.

BUILDING EMOTIONAL RESILIENCE: MAVERICKS BEYOND BUSINESS

Resilience in Maverick's Toolkit extends beyond the business realm into the emotional landscape of entrepreneurs. This chapter explores how mavericks cultivate emotional resilience to navigate the highs and lows of their journeys. Examining the personal narratives of leaders like Elon Musk, who faced public scrutiny and personal challenges, reveals how emotional fortitude becomes an integral part of the Maverick's Toolkit.

Emotional resilience is not a separate entity but an interwoven thread in the fabric of maverick success. Mavericks, despite the pressures and stresses, demonstrate a capacity to maintain focus, make decisions under duress, and emerge from challenges with a renewed sense of purpose.

THE MAVERICK'S TOOLKIT IN TIMES OF CRISIS: NAVIGATING UNCERTAINTY

The crisis is an inevitable aspect of the entrepreneurial journey. This chapter illuminates how mavericks navigate uncertainty, demonstrating a resilience that is not just reactive but proactive. Analyzing the responses of entrepreneurs like Warren Buffett and Mark Cuban during economic downturns showcases how Maverick's Toolkit is mobilized in times of crisis, transforming challenges into opportunities.

Mavericks approach crisis not with fear but with a strategic mindset. Instead of retreating, they seize the moment, identifying potential areas for growth, innovation, and market leadership. The Maverick's Toolkit becomes a beacon in times of uncertainty, guiding entrepreneurs through tumultuous waters with a steady hand and an unwavering resolve.

As we delve into the intricacies of Maverick Resilience, let's not merely dissect challenges but appreciate the transformative power embedded within them. Mavericks view adversity as a canvas on which to paint their most innovative strokes. Join me in exploring the stories of those who faced challenges head-on, embraced resilience as a guiding principle, and emerged as beacons of maverick success.

Onward we go, ready to absorb the wisdom of those

who have weathered storms, turned setbacks into stepping stones, and embraced resilience as an essential component of the Maverick's Toolkit. Welcome to Chapter 5 of "The Maverick Entrepreneur: Breaking Boundaries, Building Empires," where we unravel the profound resilience that sets mavericks apart in the entrepreneurial landscape.

CHAPTER 6
Mavericks and Society - Impact Beyond Business

In our exploration of maverick entrepreneurship, we've witnessed how these trailblazers defy norms, challenge conventions, and build empires. However, the impact of mavericks extends far beyond profit margins and market dominance; it reverberates through society, influencing culture, perceptions, and even the very fabric of our collective mindset.

REVOLUTIONIZING NORMS

Mavericks are architects of change, and Chapter 6 delves into their role in revolutionizing societal norms. From breaking gender barriers to challenging outdated stereotypes, mavericks like Cher Wang and Arianna Huffington stand as symbols of progress. Their ventures transcend business—they become catalysts for societal transformation.

Consider the impact of Richard Branson's Virgin Galactic, not just as a space tourism venture but as a symbol of human audacity and the relentless pursuit of the extraordinary. Mavericks challenge us to dream bigger, to question societal norms that may limit our potential, and to envision a world where unconventional thinking becomes the norm.

SOCIAL RESPONSIBILITY

Mavericks recognize that with great success comes a responsibility to contribute positively to society. Chapter 6 explores how these entrepreneurs leverage their influence for social good. Whether it's Elon Musk's commitment to sustainable energy or Oprah Winfrey's philanthropic endeavors, mavericks understand that their ventures can be powerful instruments for positive change.

We'll explore the stories of entrepreneurs who go beyond profit-driven motives, actively engaging in initiatives that address social issues. By examining their strategies, we gain insights into how mavericks can use their resources and influence to create a lasting impact on the world.

INSPIRING FUTURE MAVERICKS

Mavericks are not content with their success; they aim to inspire the next generation of trailblazers. This chapter unveils the mentorship initiatives, educational programs, and platforms established by Mavericks to nurture budding entrepreneurs. Mavericks recognize the importance of sharing knowledge and fostering an environment where unconventional thinking is not only accepted but celebrated.

The tales of visionary leaders mentoring aspiring entrepreneurs provide a roadmap for cultivating the maverick mindset. By understanding their commitment to education and empowerment, we gain valuable insights into how mavericks influence the future landscape of entrepreneurship.

SHAPING CULTURAL NARRATIVES

Mavericks are not just business leaders; they are cultural icons. Chapter 6 explores how their stories permeate popular culture, shaping narratives that celebrate innovation, resilience, and the pursuit of one's vision. From biographical films to media coverage, mavericks become symbols of inspiration, embodying the triumph of the human spirit against all odds.

As we journey through the impact of mavericks on society, we'll uncover the stories that showcase their role in shaping cultural narratives. These narratives not only celebrate individual success but also serve as beacons for those navigating their entrepreneurial journeys.

CHAMPIONING DIVERSITY AND INCLUSIVITY

Mavericks recognize the strength of diversity and inclusivity, and this awareness permeates their ventures. Chapter 6 delves into how these entrepreneurs champion diversity, not just within their organizations but across industries. From advocating for gender equality to fostering inclusive workplaces, mavericks amplify voices that have traditionally been marginalized.

We'll explore the stories of entrepreneurs who prioritize diversity and inclusivity, examining their strategies for breaking down barriers. Mavericks understand that diverse perspectives fuel innovation and contribute to the creation of solutions that resonate with a global audience.

ADDRESSING GLOBAL CHALLENGES

Mavericks are not content with business as usual; they confront global challenges head-on. Chapter 6 examines how these entrepreneurs leverage their resources and influence to address pressing issues such as climate change, poverty, and healthcare disparities. Mavericks understand that their ventures can be powerful instruments for positive change on a global scale.

Through the exploration of initiatives and projects led by mavericks, we gain insights into their commitment to making a meaningful impact beyond the confines of their businesses. Whether it's funding renewable energy projects, supporting education initiatives, or addressing healthcare disparities, mavericks demonstrate that business can be a force for good.

CULTURAL IMPACT THROUGH INNOVATION

Mavericks leave an indelible mark on culture through their innovative ventures. Chapter 6 delves into how their creations become cultural phenomena, influencing not only consumer behavior but also societal narratives. From groundbreaking technology to revolutionary business models, mavericks redefine the way we live, work, and interact.

Consider the cultural impact of Apple under Steve Jobs, where the introduction of products like the iPhone not only transformed the tech industry but also reshaped how we communicate and experience the world. Mavericks understand that innovation is not just about products; it's about creating experiences that resonate with the cultural zeitgeist.

EDUCATIONAL INITIATIVES

Mavericks are committed to shaping the future by investing in education. Chapter 6 explores how these entrepreneurs establish educational initiatives, scholarships, and programs aimed at empowering the next generation. Mavericks recognize that education is a cornerstone for societal progress, and their contributions extend beyond their immediate ventures.

We'll delve into the stories of entrepreneurs who prioritize education, examining their initiatives to support learning and skill development. Mavericks understand that by investing in education, they contribute to the cultivation of a skilled workforce and foster innovation for years to come.

CIVIC ENGAGEMENT AND ADVOCACY

Mavericks are not bystanders in societal issues; they actively engage in advocacy and civic initiatives. Chapter 6 explores how these entrepreneurs use their influence to champion causes ranging from social justice to political reform. Mavericks understand that their voices can amplify important messages and drive positive change.

Through the examination of their advocacy efforts, we gain insights into how mavericks navigate the intersection of business and societal impact. Whether it's speaking out on environmental issues or supporting movements for equality, mavericks recognize the role they play in shaping the broader socio-political landscape.

CULTIVATING A MAVERICK MINDSET IN SOCIETY

As we conclude our exploration of the societal impact of mavericks, Chapter 6 explores how these entrepreneurs contribute to cultivating a maverick mindset in society at large. Mavericks inspire a shift in mindset, encouraging individuals to embrace innovation, challenge norms, and pursue audacious goals.

Through their stories, initiatives, and advocacy, mavericks become catalysts for a cultural shift that values creativity, resilience, and the courage to forge new paths. This chapter examines the ripple effect of the maverick mindset, inspiring a generation to think beyond constraints and envision a future where unconventional thinking is not only accepted but celebrated.

Join me in this expansive journey through the societal impact of maverick entrepreneurs. From championing diversity and inclusivity to addressing global challenges, these entrepreneurs go beyond the traditional boundaries of business, shaping a world where audacity and innovation lead to lasting positive change. Welcome to Chapter 6 of "The Maverick Entrepreneur: Breaking Boundaries, Building Empires," where we explored the profound influence of mavericks beyond the boardroom, leaving an enduring legacy on society.

CHAPTER 7
Mavericks in the Making: Cultivating an Entrepreneurial Spirit

As our journey through the world of maverick entrepreneurship unfolds, Chapter 7 turns the spotlight on the budding visionaries, the aspiring entrepreneurs, and the dreamers who are poised to become the mavericks of tomorrow. This chapter is a roadmap, a guide to cultivating an entrepreneurial spirit and instilling the audacious mindset that defines mavericks.

IGNITING THE SPARK

Mavericks are not born; they are shaped by experiences, inspiration, and a burning desire to make a difference. Chapter 7 explores the various sources of inspiration that ignite the spark within individuals, setting them on a path of entrepreneurial exploration. From personal experiences to encounters with influential figures, these sparks have the potential to kindle the flame of innovation.

We'll delve into stories of individuals who found inspiration in unexpected places, uncovering how their unique journeys led them to embrace the entrepreneurial spirit. Mavericks in the making often draw from a diverse array of influences, and understanding these catalysts provides invaluable insights for those embarking on their entrepreneurial quests.

EDUCATIONAL FOUNDATIONS

Education is a cornerstone for aspiring mavericks, providing not only knowledge but also the tools to navigate the complex terrain of entrepreneurship. Chapter 7 explores the role of educational institutions, mentorship programs, and skill development initiatives in nurturing the entrepreneurial spirit. Mavericks in the making understand that a solid educational foundation is key to transforming ideas into impactful ventures.

We'll unravel stories of entrepreneurs who found guidance and support through educational initiatives, showcasing how these experiences shaped their journeys. From formal education to hands-on learning, the entrepreneurial spirit thrives in environments that encourage curiosity, critical thinking, and a willingness to embrace challenges.

EMBRACING FAILURE AS A STEPPING STONE

Failure is not the end; it's a crucial stepping stone on the path to maverick success. Chapter 7 delves into the mindset that views failure not as a setback but as a valuable learning experience. Mavericks in the making understand that each failure brings insights, resilience, and the opportunity to iterate towards greater success.

Through stories of entrepreneurs who faced setbacks and emerged stronger, we'll explore the transformative power of embracing failure. The maverick mindset is forged in the crucible of challenges, and understanding how to navigate and learn from failures is a fundamental aspect of cultivating an entrepreneurial spirit.

ENCOURAGING CREATIVE THINKING

Mavericks are known for their ability to think outside the box, to envision possibilities where others see limitations. Chapter 7 explores strategies for encouraging and fostering creative thinking among aspiring entrepreneurs. From innovation challenges to collaborative projects, the entrepreneurial spirit thrives in environments that prioritize and celebrate creative exploration.

We'll uncover stories of individuals who harnessed their creative thinking to solve problems, disrupt industries, and carve out their entrepreneurial paths. Creative thinking is not a talent reserved for a select few; it's a skill that can be nurtured and honed, laying the groundwork for a maverick mindset.

CULTIVATING RESILIENCE AND GRIT

The entrepreneurial journey is often fraught with challenges, requiring resilience and grit to persevere. Chapter 7 delves into the importance of cultivating these qualities, exploring how mavericks in the making navigate setbacks, rejection, and adversity. Mavericks understand that resilience is the armor that shields them in the face of uncertainty.

Through stories of entrepreneurs who overcame formidable obstacles, we'll unravel the threads of resilience and grit woven into the fabric of the maverick mindset. The ability to bounce back from setbacks, learn from failures, and persist in the pursuit of goals is a defining characteristic of those destined to become mavericks.

BUILDING A SUPPORTIVE ECOSYSTEM

No maverick succeeds in isolation; they thrive in supportive ecosystems that nurture their growth. Chapter 7 examines the role of communities, networks, and mentorship in shaping the entrepreneurial spirit. Mavericks in the making seek out environments where ideas are exchanged, collaboration is encouraged, and mentorship provides guidance.

We'll explore stories of individuals who found their entrepreneurial tribe, illustrating how a supportive ecosystem can be a catalyst for success. Building connections, seeking mentorship, and participating in entrepreneurial communities are integral components of cultivating a maverick mindset.

ADOPTING AN ITERATIVE MINDSET

Mavericks understand the power of iteration, the process of continuous improvement and refinement. Chapter 7 explores the mindset that embraces iteration as a means of evolving ideas and ventures. Mavericks in the making recognize that success often involves adapting, learning, and refining their approaches based on feedback and changing circumstances.

Through stories of entrepreneurs who iterated their way to success, we'll uncover the principles of an iterative mindset. Whether refining a business model, enhancing a product, or adjusting strategies, the ability to iterate is a hallmark of the maverick spirit.

EMPOWERING DIVERSE PERSPECTIVES

The maverick mindset thrives in environments that value diverse perspectives and experiences. Chapter 7 delves into the importance of inclusivity and diversity in fostering an entrepreneurial spirit. Mavericks in the making understand that diverse teams bring a breadth of insights, creativity, and innovative thinking.

We'll explore stories of entrepreneurs who actively seek diversity in their ventures, illustrating how varied perspectives contribute to robust problem-solving and innovation. The entrepreneurial spirit is not confined by boundaries; it flourishes in environments that embrace and celebrate differences.

STRATEGIC RISK-TAKING

Calculated risk-taking is a cornerstone of the maverick mindset. Chapter 7 explores how aspiring entrepreneurs can develop the ability to take strategic risks, understanding that innovation often involves stepping into the unknown. Mavericks in the making recognize that calculated risks are opportunities for growth and transformation.

Through stories of entrepreneurs who navigated strategic risks, we'll uncover the principles of informed decision-making in the face of uncertainty. The entrepreneurial spirit is not about reckless gambles but about carefully calculated moves that propel ventures forward.

NURTURING AN ENTREPRENEURIAL SPIRIT IN EDUCATION

As we conclude Chapter 7, we turn our attention to the role of educational institutions in nurturing the entrepreneurial spirit. From fostering innovation to providing mentorship, educational settings play a pivotal role in shaping the mavericks of tomorrow.

We'll explore innovative educational programs, initiatives, and approaches that empower students to embrace entrepreneurship. Whether through experiential learning, incubator programs, or interdisciplinary courses, these educational endeavors provide fertile ground for the cultivation of a maverick mindset.

We unraveled the journey of Mavericks in the Making. This chapter is a guide for aspiring entrepreneurs, dreamers, and visionaries eager to cultivate the audacious spirit that defines mavericks. Welcome to a chapter that inspires and empowers the next generation of trailblazers, laying the foundation for a future where bold ideas and unconventional thinking shape the entrepreneurial landscape.

CONCLUSION
Forging Mavericks, Shaping Futures

As we bring our exploration of maverick entrepreneurship to a close, the journey has been a tapestry woven with audacity, innovation, and the relentless pursuit of transformative impact. From the inception of audacious ideas to the societal resonance of maverick endeavors, the narrative unfolds not merely as a chronicle of business triumphs but as a testament to the enduring legacy of those who dared to be different.

THE MAVERICK MINDSET

At the heart of our exploration lies the Maverick Mindset—an audacious spirit that defies convention, challenges norms, and envisions possibilities where others see limitations. Mavericks are not bound by the status quo; they are architects of change, wielding innovation as a tool to reshape industries and influence society.

Throughout our journey, we've unraveled the principles that define the Maverick Mindset—from disruptive innovation to strategic risk-taking, from storytelling prowess to adaptive leadership. Mavericks navigate the entrepreneurial landscape with an unyielding belief in the transformative power of their ideas and an unwavering commitment to forging new paths.

SOCIETAL IMPACT

Beyond boardrooms and profit margins, mavericks cast a profound impact on society. Chapter after chapter, we've witnessed how their ventures transcend business—they become cultural phenomena, catalysts for societal transformation, and agents of positive change. Mavericks champion diversity, address global challenges, and inspire future generations to embrace innovation and audacity.

In the realm of maverick entrepreneurship, social responsibility is not a choice but a guiding principle. Mavericks recognize that their ventures wield influence far beyond economic metrics, and they leverage their resources to address pressing issues, contribute to education, and advocate for positive societal change.

THE JOURNEY OF MAVERICKS IN THE MAKING

Chapter 7 served as a guide for Mavericks in the Making —those who aspire to carve out their entrepreneurial paths, fueled by a spirit of innovation and resilience. From educational foundations to embracing failure as a stepping stone, from fostering creative thinking to building supportive ecosystems, the chapter illuminated the roadmap for cultivating the Maverick Mindset from its embryonic stages.

Mavericks in the Making recognizes that the entrepreneurial journey is not a solitary endeavor; it thrives in collaborative environments that celebrate diverse perspectives, embrace risk-taking, and encourage continuous iteration. The entrepreneurial spirit is not confined to a select few; it's a flame that can be ignited, nurtured, and passed on to future generations.

LEGACY AND CONTINUATION

As we conclude our exploration, the legacy of maverick entrepreneurship continues to unfold. The impact of Mavericks in the Making reverberates through the entrepreneurial landscape, shaping industries, challenging norms, and contributing to a future where audacious thinking is celebrated.

The journey of maverick entrepreneurship is an ongoing narrative—one that extends beyond these pages and into the ventures, ideas, and innovations yet to emerge. The Maverick Mindset is not static; it evolves, adapts, and thrives in the hands of those who dare to dream beyond the ordinary.

THE INVITATION

To those embarking on their entrepreneurial journeys, to the dreamers and visionaries of tomorrow, the invitation is clear: embrace the Maverick Mindset. Seize the audacious spirit that propels innovation, challenge the norms that constrain possibilities, and envision a future where your ideas shape not only industries but the very fabric of society.

As we conclude this journey, may it serve as both inspiration and guide—an exploration of the Maverick Mindset and its enduring impact on entrepreneurship and society. Welcome to the world of Mavericks, where the extraordinary is not an exception but a guiding principle, and the audacious spirit lights the way for those who dare to shape the future.

www.ingramcontent.com/pod-product-compliance
Lightning Source LLC
Chambersburg PA
CBHW050053260726
48658CB00005B/1921